SONOMA

CALIFORNIA

BY MJ ALLEN / PHOTOGRAPHS BY CATHY STANCIL

ILLUSTRATIONS BY MARK ZALL

➤ | **portrait of a town**

ISBN 0-9785217-0-6

ISBN 978-0-9785217-0-7

10 09 08 07 06   1 2 3 4 5

OCULUS CREATIVE

164 West Spain Street / Suite B

Sonoma, CA 95476

www.oculuscreative.com

For the past several summers, my family and I have hosted a child from the contaminated regions around Chernobyl, Ukraine. Before he left us to return home each year, I searched in vain for a book that he could take with him to show his family where he had spent his six weeks. I wanted something small and light that he could carry home. Something very visual and picturesque, as his family cannot read English. Something that attempted to show at least a small amount of the beauty and magic that is Sonoma.

This is that book.

Lovingly dedicated to the Astepenka family of Mozyr, Belarus.

MJ ALLEN

Sonoma has been my home away from home for the past fifteen years, and still today, I can turn a corner and be struck by the beauty I see. Creating this book enables me to share this beauty with you, and with my friends and family around the world.

Pour Maman, Claude et ma famille qui me manquent énormément.

CATHY STANCIL

SONOMA/ **an overview**

A visit to Sonoma, at its best, is like going home. When you arrive in the historic town, nestled among grapevines and sweeping mountains, you are reminded of a favorite childhood memory. You'll recall comfort and security, and food and drink in abundance. Life here is familiar and easy, beautiful and warm.

At anything less than its best, a visit to Sonoma is like watching a travelogue in which the moving images tell the story of beauty and charm, history and pioneer spirit. Every scene is picturesque and around every corner another delightful story is revealed.

Sonoma is significant in so many ways. It is rife with California history and, of course, it is ripe with grapes. It is, after all, the birthplace of winemaking in the state.

Many of the photographs in this book are of easily-recognizable places and scenes that make the town special – others are of hidden treasures that you will want to discover with each returning visit. All will elicit a fond memory of the unique spirit that is Sonoma. We hope you enjoy this portrait.

As in that perfect memory from our childhood, often we have a special place where family and friends gathered. To eat, to play, or simply to be. It was the spot where we came together to watch and listen and share. It was the heart of our world. Sonoma too has that heart. It is *The Plaza*, a National Historic Landmark since 1961 and the largest

of its kind in the state. It has always served as the town's focal point, hosting community festivals and social gatherings year round. It is an eight-acre park filled with stately trees and pedestrian pathways and is surrounded on four sides by shops, restaurants, and historic sites. Directly at its center is the early 20th-century City Hall *(far right, top.)* It is still in use today, and a reminder of the town's early California history.

Sonoma Plaza

One of the most prominent icons on the Sonoma Plaza is the Sebastiani Theater *(left.)* It was built in 1933 by August Sebastiani as a movie house. Now it is used as a venue for everything from live performances to independent films and blockbuster movies. It serves as center stage for *Cinema Epicuria*, the Sonoma Valley Film Festival that, as with most celebrations in Sonoma, combines the love of art with the love of food and wine.

Leading off of The Plaza, on all four sides of the square, are numerous pedestrian alleys *(right)* full of shops and restaurants – all begging to be explored.

Sonoma Plaza

The mission in Sonoma was founded in 1823 when a Franciscan Father, Jose Altimira, declared Sonoma Valley the most beautiful site he could imagine for a mission dedicated to God's work. Thus began the building of Mission San Francisco Solano. It was the last

and northern-most mission built in California and the only one founded after Mexico's independence from Spain. It was named after St. Francis of Solano, a 17th century missionary to the Peruvian Indians. It is referred to today simply as Mission Sonoma.

The Mission

During the 1500's, Spain claimed a vast area of land along the western side of North America. This land was rich, fertile and near the sea. It was the perfect place to build cities and harbors. 200 years later, in 1768, in an attempt to keep that area under Spanish rule, King Charles III of Spain sent Franciscan priests to colonize the valuable land. And that, consequently, began the development of the California Mission system. The Franciscan priests moved into these idyllic places, attempted to convert the non-Christian natives from

the area, provide them with food, water and shelter, and use them to build the missions and tend the fields. It was most definitely through the Indian's efforts that the priests were able to accomplish what would have otherwise been an impossible task. Missions were built every four years or so up and down the California coast for the next 50 years. They eventually reached from San Diego in the south to Sonoma in the north – with 21 missions in all. Today they commemorate a rich and volatile period in California history.

SAN FRANCISCO SONOMA, 1823

SONOMA

SAN RAFAEL ARCANGEL, 1817

SAN FRANCISCO DE ASIS, 1776

FRANCISCO

SANTA CLARA DE ASIS, 1777

SAN JOSE, 1777

SANTA CRUZ, 1791

MONTEREY

SAN JUAN BAUTISTA, 1797

SAN CARLOS BORROMEO DE CARMELO, 1770

NUESTRA SENORA DE LA SOLEDAD, 1791

CALIFORNIA

SAN ANTONIO DE PADUA, 1771

SAN MIGUEL ARCHANGEL, 1797

SAN LUIS OBISPO DE TOLOSA, 1772

MISSIONS

LA PURISIMA CONCEPCION, 1787

SANTA INES, 1804

SANTA BARBARA, 1786

SANTA BARBARA

SAN BUENAVENTURA, 1782

MAP

SAN FERNANDO REY DE ESPANA, 1797

LOS ANGELES

SAN GABRIEL ARCANGEL, 1771

SAN JUAN CAPISTRANO, 1776

SAN LUIS RAY DE FRANCIS, 1798

SAN DIEGO

SAN DIEGO DE ALCALA, 1769

onoma played many
fluential roles in California
story. In the early 1800's,
alifornia was a part of Mexico,
nown as Alta California. But
n June 14, 1846, without
nowing that war had already
een declared between the
nited States and Mexico,
group of local hunters and
appers took over General
ariano Vallejo's headquarters
Sonoma. They proclaimed
independent "Republic
California" and created a
g with a grizzly bear and
single red star. And for 25
ys, Sonoma served as
e capital of that Republic.
is conflict became known
The Bear Flag Revolt.
nerican forces arrived in
onoma soon thereafter,
ushing the Republic, but
lidifying California's destiny
becoming a future part of
e United States.

Once a year
the Historic Society
of Sonoma performs
a reenactment of
The Bear Flag Revolt,
depicted here
in these photos

History

The town of Sonoma has gracefully maintained the heritage of its early years. There are countless historic buildings and relics sprinkled in and around The Plaza. The Toscano Hotel, being one of them *(below,)* was built in 1851, and is the oldest commercial wood-frame structure in Sonoma. Today it is furnished with period furniture

and looks much the way it did around the turn of the century. The adobe barracks *(page 15 and near right)* face Sonoma Plaza. They were built in 1836 to house Mexican army troops under the command of General Vallejo and in 1846 they became the headquarters of the Bear Flag Party.

Four blocks away, in 1851, General Vallejo built his family home *(a portion of which is shown above.)* He called it Lachryma Montis — Latin for *tears of the mountains* — after the local Indian name for a spring on the property that they called "crying mountain." The house was built in the grand Gothic Revival style, popular during that period.

The Land

The town of Sonoma sits at the southeastern corner of the lush Sonoma Valley far away from any major thoroughfares or freeways. Perhaps that is one reason for its unspoiled countenance. The valley itself is approximately 17 miles long with hundreds of acres of vineyards and farmland and is nestled between the Sonoma Mountain Range on the west and the Mayacamas on the east.

The importance of land in this valley cannot be emphasized too strongly. It is the lifeline that feeds and nourishes, both literally and figuratively, so many of the people who live and work in this region. When nurtured, the land provides in abundance. And when unattended, it affords us the opportunity of seeing the magnificence and beauty in nature.

The Land

Wine

The Sonoma Valley is the birthplace of the California premium wine industry. It was the Franciscan mission fathers who first planted the vineyards here in 1824. But in 1857, Count Agoston Haraszthy from Hungary purchased Salvador Vallejo's vineyard in Sonoma, renamed it Buena Vista, and planted the first major vineyard of European varietals.

Today many of the
world's finest wines
continue to be
produced in Sonoma
Valley where the artistry
of winemaking has
become both a
business and a lifestyle.

Wine

Sonoma Valley is a federally designated wine appellation region, which begins in the north at the edge of Santa Rosa and extends 17 miles south to include the Carneros area above San Pablo Bay. Many grape varietals are grown in the Valley – all thriving in very specific conditions, unique to each area. For instance, in the cooler Carneros area, wineries grow early-ripening varieties such as Chardonnay, Pinot Noir, and Merlot. In the warmer areas, along the hillsides and the valley floor, Zinfandel and Cabernet Sauvignon flourish.

A list of Sonoma Valley Wineries with addresses and phone numbers are listed on page 68.

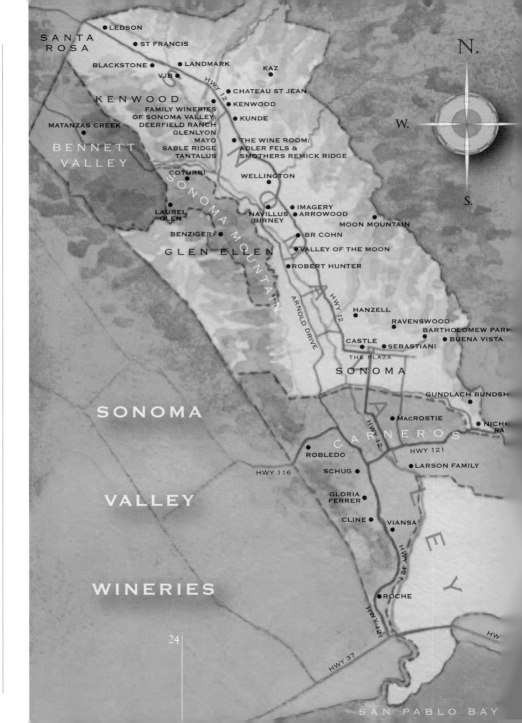

There are more than 60 wineries in Sonoma Valley. Viansa Winery *(left)* with its tile-roofed Tuscan Villa sits atop a hill surrounded by olive trees, vineyards and a 90-acre waterfowl preserve. Cline Cellars *(below left)* is on a historic 350-acre estate, once the site of a Miwok Indian village.

Wine

Wineries in the valley are as diverse and unique as the varietals they produce. Each has a particular personality, some based on heritage, some on proximity to a unique location, some on the vision of the winemaker or owner. Shown this page, (*clockwise from top left*) are the Benziger Hospitality Room; The entrance to Ravenswood Winery; The front steps to Bartholomew Park Winery; and the historic wooden doors to Sebastiani Winery. One of the newer wineries to be built is Nicholson Ranch Winery (*opposite page/top.*) And in contrast is Buena Vista Winery (*opposite page/ bottom*) the first premium winery founded in the state in 1857 by Count Agoston Haraszthy.

Food

Good food is synonymous with Sonoma. The town is filled with first-class restaurants and specialty food shops, many influenced by fresh, local ingredients including the abundance of organic products grown in the valley. Cafe La Haye *(left)* is a small restaurant of 14 tables, just off The Plaza, with a relaxed, but chic atmosphere. Vella Cheese Company *(opposite/inset)* has been producing award-winning, carefully crafted cheese since 1931. Today it continues to make cheese in the original stonewall building where it all started. The Cheesemaker's Daughter *(far right)* is run by proprietress Ditty Vella, who grew up in the Vella Cheese Company family. Although her roots are in American cheeses, the shop offers a wonderful variety of fine European artisanal cheeses as well.

29

Food

(Shown opposite page, clockwise from top left:) The garden patio at Della Santina's Trattoria; the General's Daughter, so named because it is the former home of one of General Vallejo's daughters, Natalia; The Swiss Hotel with outdoor seating on The Plaza; and The Girl and the Fig, a charming and colorful restaurant with original art by Julie Higgins. *(This page)* Cucina Rustica, located in the Depot Hotel, a beautifully restored plumstone building, once the local hotel for 19th century passengers arriving on the train from San Francisco.

A list of Sonoma Restaurants with addresses and phone numbers are listed on page 67.

(Shown this page:) The interior dinning room of Della Santina's Trattoria. Because of the near-perfect weather conditions of the Sonoma Valley, most establishments provide indoor and outdoor seating. *(Shown Opposite:)* Details of some of the many fruits and vegetables sold at the Friday morning farmer's market.

The opening of Ramekins in 1998 continued Sonoma's love affair with glorious food. The school celebrates locally grown ingredients by teaching home cooks how to prepare them simply and deliciously. The school draws well-known chefs and cookbook authors to Sonoma to lead classes.

Art

Sonomans celebrate art, as evidence by the many shows and festivals that support the fine arts year round. *Sonoma Plein Air* is one such festival. It is a weeklong event celebrating the century-old technique of outdoor painting. Plein-air, a French expression that translates as "open air,"

describes painting done outdoors, on location. Unlike earlier landscape artists, the goal of late 19th-century French pleinairistes, was to capture an impression of the fleeting effects of natural light. Above are examples of local plein air artists. *(Clockwise from top left)* Anne Hysell, "*Pink Hills," 2002, pastels;* Dick Cole, "*Fixer Upper," 2000, watercolor;* Keith Wicks, "*Sonoma Road," 2004, oils;* Dennis Ziemienski, "The *Chocolate Barn," 2005, oils.*

In 1998, the residents of Sonoma began to explore the possibilities of establishing a fine arts museum in Sonoma. That dream came to fruition, when in 2004, a newly remodeled museum opened its doors. Since then The Sonoma Valley Museum of Art has exhibited internationally renowned artists as well as artists of historic importance and, of course, local favorites.

To many who live in Sonoma, art is a way of life. The town is a haven for prominent painters, sculptures, woodworkers, architects, filmmakers and more. And art is found just about everywhere, from restaurants to building murals, from galleries to sculpture gardens, from the side of roads to private collections. *(Opposite page:) "The Blue Tree,"* by Claude Cormier (covered in 70,000 plastic balls,) Cornerstone Festival of Gardens; *(This page/from top:) "Lucille The Cow,"* private collection; *"Stone Grapes,"* Ron Mann Design; *"Flowers"* from the Ira Wolk Collection, MacArthur Place Garden Gallery.

Many of the buildings in Sonoma are either original abobe structures, or inspired by that movement. Adobe is a building material composed of water, sandy clay and straw or other organic materials, which is shaped into bricks and dried in the sun. The Franciscan fathers used the ancient technique when building the missions, owing both to the limited selection of building materials available, and an overall lack of advanced construction experience. Adobe structures are extremely durable and offer significant advantages in hot, dry climates, because they remain cooler as the bricks store and release heat very slowly.

Architecture

Today there are remnants of many different architectural styles prevalent in Sonoma. They range from Gothic Revival to Queen Anne to Spanish Colonial. It's the wonderful mixture of historic styles and techniques that gives the town it's eclectic and unique architectural feel. Walk a couple bocks east from The Plaza to see some of the more scenic homes and buildings. One such building is The Blue Wing Inn *(below/left.)* It was built by General Vallejo around 1840 to accommodate emigrants and other travelers and was among the first hotels in Northern California

Natural Beauty

No wonder the Franciscan priests found Sonoma to be the perfect spot for developing their mission. It has a temperate climate year-round, plenty of water, and natural beauty in excess. Even on cool gray mornings, when the fog is trapped in the valley by the Sonoma Mountains, there is a majestic beauty to the way the light reflects off the leaves or the way the bird's call is slightly softened by the blanket of moisture.

Natural Beauty

Sonoma is a place to be outdoors. To enjoy the wildflowers, the extensive hiking trails, the array of birds and other wildlife. *(Shown opposite page:)* The lavender fields, in full bloom, at Rock Hill Estate.

Beauty comes in many forms. And nowhere is that more evident than in the various neighborhoods around Sonoma. If you get off the beaten path, you'll discover the hidden gems that make the town so wonderfully diverse. One of those gems, the Hispanic culture,

permeates the streets of rural Boyes Hot Springs and Agua Caliente. You'll find the traditions of Mexico in the color, sounds and energy of those neighborhoods. You'll taste it in the authentic Mexican food and drink sold at small mercados and restaurants.

Unique Spirit

The spirit of Sonoma, found in the people who live here, is a simple reflection of the many places and things that are considered important and meaningful. It is a reflection of what makes Sonomans tick, what makes them happy, and ultimately, what makes the town, itself, so special. (Too many to mention all,) here are but a few of those things: **Music.** In The Plaza amphitheater on a hot summer night *(above/right;)* at Murphy's Irish Pub; at the Sonoma Jazz festival; at the Cinco de Mayo celebration *(below/right;)* or at a performance by The Hometown Band. **4th of July Celebration.** *(opposite)* Sonomans truly know how to do a parade. Old-fashioned fun. Add lots of water.

Thermal mineral waters. The areas around Sonoma have been blessed with natural mineral springs. And there is no better place to enjoy them than at Fairmont Sonoma Mission Inn and Spa *(left,)* a luxury resort with first-class accommodations and facilities.

Little Switzerland. Experience the feeling of a 1920's beer garden while you dance the night away at the "greatest dance hall in Northern California."

Sonoma Train Town

(this page.) The most well-developed scale railroad in the Americas! Yes, it's true. And it's in Sonoma.

Food and Wine Festivals. One of the finest is the Olive Festival *(top/left)* where all things olive are celebrated and enjoyed*;* **Sonoma Mission Gardens.** *(top/right)* The best nursery in town to replant, reshape or reinvigorate your garden; **Anne Appleman Flowers and Plants.** One of the most charming and creative flower shops anywhere. **The Mountain Cemetery.** *(bottom/right)* Spend hours strolling among the graves of some of Sonoma's early pioneers, including General Vallejo himself. T**he Avalon Players.** Directed by Kate Kennedy. *(bottom/left)* Catch a superb Shakespeare production under the stars at Gundlach Bundschu Winery.

Tuesday Night Markets.

(right) Every Tuesday evening during the summer months, from 5:00 until dusk, enjoy live music, organic produce and baked goods, fresh-cut flowers and almost anything else you can imagine. Bring a blanket and a chair and bottle of wine and watch the hundreds of people who turn out each week.

Unique Spirit

A Hike at Bartholomew Park Winery. *(top/left)* Enjoy a hearty walk through vineyards **and** redwood groves, across streams and up to spectacular vistas; **Sonoma Community Center.** *(top/right)* A former elementary school that now offers theatrical and live performances, art and music classes, local events and much more; **Readers' Books.** *(bottom/right)* Take a stroll a half block from The Plaza and discover Readers', Sonoma's literary gathering place. You'll find good books, good talk, lots of events, plus opinions, jokes, and music in abundance. **Local Theatrical Productions.** *(bottom/left and opposite)* At almost any given time, you can find heart-warming musicals, plays, and ballets being performed by Sonoma's very own.

We hope that in some small way this book will help you to remember, with fondness, the time you spent in Sonoma. However, we know that nothing really compares to the actual experience. So savor your visit, and return often.

THANKS SO MUCH TO THE FOLLOWING PEOPLE.

FOR HER FRIENDSHIP AND
EDITING ABILITY EXTRAORDINAIRE:
Janet Keeler

FOR THEIR INVALUABLE KNOWLEGE AND ADVICE:
Charles Allen
Todd McCartney
Dave Brummett and Micaelia Randolph
Andy and Lilla Weinberger

AND FOR THEIR LOVE, PATIENCE AND SUPPORT:
James, Maëva and Margaux
Mark, Maddie and Jack

This book is, by no means, meant to be a comprehensive guide of Sonoma.
It is, instead, our vision of this town...what makes it so special and what we love about it.
We apologize if we have inadvertently left anyone or anything out who feels they
should have been included. That was not our intent.

Local Listings

Anne Appleman Flowers and Plants
707-938-357
147 East Spain Street

The Avalon Players
707-938-5277
2000 Denmark Street

Little Switzerland
938-9990
19080 Riverside Drive

Murphy's Irish Pub
707-935-0660
464 First Street

Readers' Books
707-939-1779
130 East Napa Street

The Sebastiani Theater
707-996-2020
476 First Street East

Sonoma Community Center
707-938-4626
276 East Napa Street

Sonoma Mission Gardens Nursery
707-938-5775
851 Craig Avenue

Sonoma Train Town
707-938-3912
20264 Broadway Street

Sonoma Valley Visitors Bureau
707-996-1090
453 First Street East

Sonoma Hotels

El Dorado Hotel
707-996-3030
405 First Street West

El Pueblo Inn
707-996-3651
896 West Napa Street

Fairmont Sonoma Mission Inn & Spa
707-938-9000
18140 Sonoma Highway

Ledson Hotel & Harmony Club
707-996-9779
480 First Street East

Lodge at Sonoma
707-935-6600
1325 Broadway

MacArthur Place Inn & Spa
707-938-2929
29 East MacArthur Street

Sonoma Hotel
707-996-2996
110 West Spain Street

Sonoma Valley Inn
707-938-9200
550 West Second Street

Swiss Hotel
707-938-2884
18 West Spain St.

Sonoma Bed & Breakfasts

Bungalows 313
707-996-8091
313 First Street East

Cooperage Inn
707-996-7054
301 First Street West

Cottage Inn & Spa
707-996-0719/800-944-1490
302 First Street East

Donner Cottage
707-996-2482
270 France Street

Ericksen's
707-938-4654
851 Second Street East

Hidden Oak Inn
707-996-9863
214 East Napa Street

Inn at Sonoma
888-568-9818
630 Broadway

Ramekins
707-933-0452
450 West Spain Street

Sonoma Chalet
707-938-3129
18935 Fifth Street West

Stonegrove
707-939-8249
240 Second Street East

Thistle Dew Inn
707-938-2909 or 800-382-789:
171 West Spain Street

Trojan Horse Inn
800-899-1925
19455 Sonoma Highway

Victorian Garden Inn
800-543-5339
316 East Napa Street

THE LODGE AT SONOMA

COTTAGE INN AND SPA

MACARTHUR PLACE

Sonoma Restaurants

Amigos Grill & Cantina
707-939-0743
19315 Sonoma Highway

Basque Boulangerie
707-935-7687
460 First Street East

Breakaway Cafe
707-996-5949
19101 Sonoma Highway

Cafe La Haye
707-935-5994
140 East Napa Street

Carneros Bistro & Wine Bar
at the Sonoma Lodge
707-931-2042
1325 Broadway

Della Santina's Trattoria
707-935-0576
133 East Napa Street

Depot Hotel - Cucina Rustica
707-938-2980
241 First Street West

Deuce
707-933-3823
691 Broadway

El Dorado Kitchen
707-996-3030
405 First Street West

The General's Daughter
707-938-4004
400 West Spain Street

The Girl and the Fig
707-938-3634
110 West Spain Street

Harmony Club
at the Ledson Hotel
707-996-9779
480 First Street East

Juanita Juanita
707-935-3981
19114 Arnold Drive

La Casa Restaurant & Bar
707-938-1866
121 East Spain Street

LaSalette
707-938-1927
452 First Street East, Suite H

Mary's Pizza Shack
707-938-3600
18636 Sonoma Highway

Mary's Pizza Shack
707-938-8300
Sonoma Plaza on Spain Street

Maya
935-3500
101 East Napa Street

**Meritâge Martini Oyster
Bar & Grille**
707-938-9430
165 West Napa Street

Murphy's Irish Pub
935-0660
464 First Street East

Pizzeria Capri Ristorante
707-935-6805
1266 Broadway

Pearl's Diner
707-996-1783
561 Fifth Street West

The Red Grape
707-996-4103
529 First Street West

Rin's Thai Restaurant
707-938-1462
139 East Napa Street

Saddles Steakhouse
at MacArthur Place
707-933-3191
29 East MacArthur Street

Sante at the Fairmont
Sonoma Mission Inn & Spa
707-938-9000
18140 Sonoma Hwy

Schellville Grill
707-996-5151
22900 Broadway

Sonoma Cheese Factory
707-996-1931
2 West Spain Street

Sunflower Caffe
707-996-6645
421 First Street West

Swiss Hotel
707-938-2884
18 West Spain Street

Taste of the Himalayas
707-996-1161
464 First Street East

THE SWISS HOTEL

Sonoma Valley Wineries *(Address in Sonoma unless otherwise specified)*

Adler Fels Winery
707-539-3123
5325 Corrick Lane, Santa Rosa

Arrowood Vineyards & Winery
800-935-2600
14347 Sonoma Hwy, Glen Ellen

Audelssa Estate Winery
707-996-1790
2992 Cavedale Road, Glen Ellen

B.R. Cohn Winery
800-330-4064 ext. 24
15000 Sonoma Highway, Glen Ellen

Batholomew Park Winery
707-935-9511
1000 Vineyard Lane

Benziger Family Winery
888-490-2739
1883 London Ranch Rd., Glen Ellen

Blackstone Winery
707-833-1999
8450 Sonoma Highway, Kenwood

Buena Vista Carneros
707-265-1472
18000 Old Winery Road

Castle Vineyards & Winery
707-996-1966
122 West Spain Street

Charles Creek Vineyard
707-935-3848
483 1st Street West

Chateau St. Jean
707-833-4134
8555 Sonoma Hwy, Kenwood

Cline Cellars
707-935-4310
24737 Arnold Dr. (Hwy 121)

Coturri Winery
707-525-9126
PO Box 396, Glen Ellen

GlenLyon Vineyards & Winery
707-833-0032
PO Box 1329, Glen Ellen

Gloria Ferrer
707-996-7256
23555 Hwy. 121

Gundlach Bundschu Winery
707-938-5277
2000 Denmark Street

Hanzell Vineyards
707-996-3860
18596 Lomita Ave.

Imagery Estate Winery
707-935-4500
14335 Highway 12, Glen Ellen

Kamen Estate Wines
707-933-1700
P.O Box 1404

Kaz Vineyard & Winery
707-833-2536
233 Adobe Canyon Rd., Kenwood

Kenwood Vineyards
707-833-5891
9592 Sonoma Hwy., Kenwood

Kunde Estate Winery & Vineyards
707-833-5501
10155 Sonoma Hwy., Kenwood

Landmark Vineyards
707-833-0053
101 Adobe Canyon Rd., Kenwood

Larson Family Winery
707-938-3031
23355 Millerick Road

Laurel Glen
707-526-3914
Box 1419, Glen Ellen

Ledson Winery & Vineyards
707-833-2330
7335 Sonoma Hwy., Kenwood

Little Vineyards
707-996-2750
15188 Sonoma Hwy., Glen Ellen

MacRostie Winery & Vineyards
707-996-4480
PO Box 340

Matanzas Creek Winery
707-528-6464
6097 Bennett Valley Road, Santa Rosa

Mayo Family Winery
707-938-9401
13101 Arnold Drive, Glen Ellen

Moon Mountain Vineyards
707-996-5870
1700 Moon Mountain Road

Muscardini Cellars
707-933-9305
17030 Park Avenue

Navillus Birney Winery
707-939-8514
13647 Arnold Drive, Glen Ellen

Nicholson Ranch Winery
707-938-8822
4200 Napa Road

Parmelee-Hill Vineyards
707-933-8905
1695 Sperring Road

Petroni Vineyards
707-935-8311
990 Cavedale Road

Ravenswood
707-938-1960
18701 Gehricke Road

Robert Hunter Winery
707-996-3056
15655 Arnold Drive, Glen Ellen

Robledo Family Winery
707- 939 -6903
21901 Bonness Road

Roche Carneros Estate Winery
707-935-7115
28700 Arnold Drive

S.L. Cellars
707-833-4455 / 707-833-5070
9380 Sonoma Highway, Kenwood

Sable Ridge Vineyards
707-542-3138
PO Box 889, Kenwood

Saxon Brown Wines
707-939-9530
PO Box 1832

Schug Carneros Estate Winery
707-939-9363 / 800-966-9365
602 Bonneau Rd.

Sebastiani Vineyards & Winery
707-933-3230
389 Fourth Street East

Sharp Cellars
707-933-0556
17560 Norbom Road

Smothers Remick Ridge Vineyards
707-833-1010
9575 Sonoma Highway, Kenwood

St. Francis Winery & Vineyards
800-543-7713
100 Pythian Road, Kenwood

Tantalus Winery
707-933-8218
19320 Orange Ave., Kenwood

Tin Barn Vineyards
707-938-5430
21692 Eighth Street East, Suite 340

Ty Caton Vineyards
707-938-3224
PO Box 830

Valley of the Moon Winery
707-996-6941
777 Madrone Rd., Glen Ellen

Viansa Winery & Italian Marketplace
800-995-4740
25200 Arnold Drive

VJB Vineyards & Cellars
707-833-2300
9077 Sonoma Hwy., Kenwood

Wellington Winery
707-939-0708
11600 Dunbar Rd., Glen Ellen